MILESTONES
IN MODERN SCIENCE

EINSTEIN'S
THEORIES OF RELATIVITY

Alan Morton

Evans

Published by Evans Brothers Limited
2A Portman Mansions
Chiltern Street
London W1U 6NR

British Library Cataloguing in Publication Data

Morton, Alan
Einstein's theory of relativity. - (Milestones in modern science)
   1. Einstein, Albert, 1879-1955 - Juvenile literature
   2. Relativity (Physics) - Juvenile literature
   3. Discoveries in science - Juvenile literature
   I. Title
530. 1'1

ISBN 0237527375

Consultant: Dr Anne Whitehead
Editor: Sonya Newland
Designer: D.R. Ink
Picture researcher: Julia Bird

Acknowledgements

Cover American Institute of Physics/Science Photo Library; Laguna Design/Science Photo Library; NASA/Science Photo Library 3 Mehau Kulyik/Science Photo Library 4(t) Science Museum/Science & Society Picture Library 4(b) Science Museum/Science & Society Picture Library 5 US Department of Energy/Science Photo Library 6(t) © Bettmann/Corbis 6(b) © Bettmann/Corbis 7 Science Museum/Science & Society Picture Library 8 David Hardy/Science Photo Library 9(t) Science Museum/Science & Society Picture Library 9(b) Science Museum/Science & Society Picture Library 10 Department of Physics, Imperial College/Science Photo Library 11(l) Jerry Mason/Science Photo Library 11(r) David Parker/Science Photo Library 13 © Bettmann/Corbis 14 Sheila Terry/Science Photo Library 15(t) Science Photo Library 15(b) Zephyr/Science Photo Library 16 Novosti/Science Photo Library 17 Science Photo Library 18 Science Photo Library 19(r) NASA/Science Photo Library 22(t) Philippe Plailly/Eurelios/Science Photo Library 23 David A. Hardy/Science Photo Library 24(b) Robert Brook/Science Photo Library 25 Science Museum/Science & Society Picture Library 26 Mehau Kulyik/Science Photo Library 27 Royal Observatory, Edinburgh/Science Photo Library 28(t) Sheila Terry/Science Photo Library 28(b) Laguna Design/Science Photo Library 29(b) NASA/Science Photo Library 30 Science Museum/Science & Society Picture Library 31 Science Photo Library 32 Philippe Plailly/Science Photo Library 34(t) David Parker/Science Photo Library 34(b) Science Photo Library 36(t) US Department of Energy/Science Photo Library 36(b) © Corbis 37 Science Museum/Science & Society Picture Library 38(t) CERN/Science Photo Library 38(b) Los Alamos National Laboratory/Science Photo Library 39 Scott Camazine/Science Photo Library 40 NASA/Science Photo Library 41 Mehau Kulyik/Science Photo Library 42(t) Mark Garlick/Science Photo Library 42(b) Detlev Van Ravenswaay/Science Photo Library 43 American Institute of Physics/Science Photo Library 44 NASA/Science Photo Library

CONTENTS

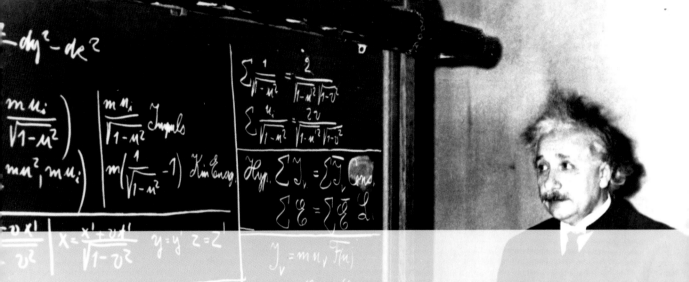

'I know quite certainly that I myself have no special talent; curiosity, obsession and dogged endurance, combined with self-criticism, have brought me to my ideas.' **ALBERT EINSTEIN**

Introduction

ABOVE: *Albert Einstein, whose theories of relativity changed the way people understood the Universe.*

BELOW: *One of the most important consequences of Einstein's theories was that they allowed scientists and astronomers to understand how gravity worked on massive bodies like stars. This is a star cluster containing thousands of stars, all held together by their mutual gravitational attraction.*

When we listen to the radio or watch television, or download music from the Internet, we take the technologies for granted. Without them society as we know it could not function. All these things are based on the understanding of the structure of matter that has been developed over the last 200 years or so, and Albert Einstein was one of the key scientists who contributed to this understanding. He spent his whole life trying to figure out some of the greatest mysteries in the Universe, from the very large to the very small.

His theories of relativity provided some of the greatest scientific leaps in the twentieth century, and they had profound implications even during his lifetime. Together with the field of science we call quantum mechanics – the study of physical phenomena on the tiniest scales (for which Einstein himself helped lay the foundations) – relativity has completely revolutionised the way we understand the Universe.

What is more amazing is that, while the best scientific brains in the world were puzzling over the then-unexplained properties of light and its relationship to mass, energy and, indeed, all physical phenomena, it was a young man working as a patent clerk in Switzerland, pondering these great questions in his spare time, who finally unlocked the secrets. From the simple process of abandoning all commonly accepted ideas about time and motion, Einstein formulated his first theory of relativity – Special Relativity – in 1905. In its most detailed form, relativity often has the cleverest scientists scratching their heads in bewilderment! However, the key predictions made by Einstein can be understood if we do the same as he did – forget what we believe to be true of time (that it is the same for everyone, wherever they are) and motion (that things are either moving or at rest). Instead of this, Einstein said that time and space are *relative* to the person observing them. In the General Theory of Relativity, published in 1915, Einstein introduced gravity into the equation and, in doing so, turned on its head everything people had previously believed about how massive bodies like the Sun move, and how they cause other bodies nearby to move – including the Earth. A whole new understanding of the Universe and how it works was demonstrated. At the opposite end of the scale, the predictions made in relativity gave rise to the field of nuclear physics – science dealing with the tiny properties of the atom. One of the most significant consequences of this was the development of nuclear weapons. In theory and in practice, relativity changed the world for ever.

BELOW: Nuclear weapons like this atomic bomb were a result of the new 'nuclear physics' that resulted from Einstein's predictions in his theories of relativity.

CHAPTER ONE

'A hundred times every day I remind myself that my inner and outer life are based on the labours of other men, living and dead, and that I must exert myself in order to give in the same measure as I have received and am still receiving.' **ALBERT EINSTEIN, 1931**

Einstein's World

ABOVE: Einstein and his first wife, Mileva. They met at the Federal Polytechnic School in Switzerland.

BELOW: Einstein with his sister Maja, when he was eight years old.

ALBERT EINSTEIN GREW UP IN EUROPE during a time of great change and development. One of the main areas in which there were major advances was science. Scientists all over Europe and in the United States were making discoveries and coming up with new inventions that changed the way people lived their everyday lives. Einstein became one of the most famous names associated with the period of investigation and discovery at the turn of the twentieth century.

EINSTEIN'S EARLY YEARS

Albert Einstein was born at Ulm in Württemberg, Germany on 14 March 1879. His father was a businessman who travelled around a lot, and when he was just a baby the family moved to Munich. Albert's parents worried about him when he was young because he did not seem to be developing very quickly. He did not begin to talk until he was three years old, and as he grew older he preferred playing alone to spending time with other children – he was very shy. He was

close to his sister and his parents, though. His mother was a great music-lover and young Albert shared her passion, learning the violin and listening to music by composers such as Mozart and Bach. His fascination with scientific questions also showed at an early age. When he was five years old, his father gave him a compass and Albert puzzled over what exactly made the needle always point towards north.

Albert's early years were spent moving from place to place and he went to several different schools in Munich (Germany), Milan (Italy) and Aarau (Switzerland). This does not seem to have hindered his education, though. Despite his late development, he loved his lessons, particularly mathematics. When his family settled permanently in Italy, Einstein decided to return to Munich to study electrical engineering. He hoped this would earn him a place at the Federal Polytechnic School, an elite technical school in Zürich, Switzerland, which would train him to become a teacher in physics and mathematics. He failed the entrance exam the first time, but in 1896 he finally gained a place. Physics was

ABOVE: *Einstein grew up at a time when industry was booming. New railways were being constructed all over Europe and the United States, and huge factories like the one shown in this painting, were used to make the necessary parts from iron and steel.*

SCIENCE FICTION

One sign of the growing importance of science and technology was the rise in what we now call science-fiction novels. In 1898 H. G. Wells published 'The War of the Worlds', in which he imagined a war between Earth and Mars. The interesting thing about this book was that in it, Wells suggested the possibility of powerful weapons that were very much like atomic bombs. At the time, scientists knew hardly anything about atoms, and it was nearly 50 years before atomic bombs were actually made.

ABOVE: An illustration of H. G. Wells' The War of the Worlds, showing technologically advanced Martians attacking a battleship on Earth.

a very new subject at the time and there was only a handful of students in his year. Here, he met and fell in love with a fellow student, Mileva Maric, who shared his passion for music and physics. They had a daughter, Lieserl, before they were married, but no one knows what happened to her. She may have died in childhood, or been adopted.

Einstein graduated from the school in 1901 and took on a few temporary teaching jobs. He had trouble finding a permanent position as a teacher, though, so he eventually accepted a job at the Swiss Patent Office in Bern, examining patent applications. In 1903 he and Mileva were married. They had two sons – Hans Albert, who went on to become a university professor, and Eduard, who inherited Einstein's love of music.

This was a busy time for Einstein. Although the job was not exactly what he wanted, he found it interesting. In the little time available to him after the demands of work and family life, Einstein continued to think about physics. He had a questioning mind, and he never simply believed what others accepted as scientific truth. This questioning of long-held beliefs in matters of physics would lead Einstein to formulate some of the most radical theories ever suggested.

NEW TECHNOLOGIES

During the time Einstein was growing up, Germany, along with Britain and France, was a leading industrial and scientific nation. Industry in the nineteenth century depended on coal. Huge amounts of steel went to build the new railways that were spreading rapidly across Europe. To make that steel, and to provide fuel for the trains, ever-increasing amounts of coal were mined.

In the last few decades of the nineteenth century another industry became just as important – the electricity industry. By 1900 the first power stations were generating electricity to provide street lighting to replace gas lamps, and for all sorts of other uses. Electricity transformed people's lives at work and in the home in the last few years of the nineteenth century and the first decade of the twentieth century, with telephones, gramophones and radios, as well as lighting. Around the same time, the first motor cars – and the first aeroplanes – came into use. The fact that scientists now understood electricity was very important – they used it in many experiments to reveal information that they would previously have been unable to discover.

Many of these new technologies were developed from research carried out in laboratories funded by governments or companies. So great was the interest in new science and technology that universities were founded to specialise in these areas. The existing universities had to keep up so they built new facilities. These became the first dedicated science laboratories for research and teaching. Even the school curriculum was changed to include science, which had rarely been taught before. Through all these innovations, governments in countries across Europe and the USA provided technical training for the men needed to work in the new science-based industries that were springing up everywhere.

RIGHT: An electrical workshop showing the wonders of electric lighting in the late eighteenth century. This workshop was owned by Joseph Swan, who invented the light bulb in England at around the same time as Thomas Edison patented it in the USA.

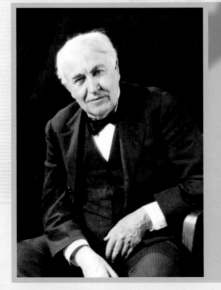

Key People

Thomas Edison (1847–1931) was the greatest inventor of the nineteenth and early twentieth centuries. Many of his inventions changed the way ordinary people lived. His most important work was with electricity. He invented the electric light bulb, and from his experiments with this he went on to create generators, light sockets, motors, fuses and many other electrical devices. The developments in this area played a major part in all manner of scientific fields. Although Edison's inventions were extremely useful in their own right, his experiments with harnessing electricity opened the way for great leaps in understanding many more fundamental problems that had been perplexing scientists for years.

CHAPTER TWO

'The most important fundamental laws and facts of physical science have all been discovered, and these are now so firmly established that the possibility of their ever being supplemented in consequence of new discoveries is exceedingly remote.' **ALBERT MICHELSON, 1894**

Ferment in Physics

BY 1900 MANY DISCOVERIES HAD BEEN MADE IN CHEMISTRY AND physics. But as scientists solved some of the mysteries, they found that new questions arose. For example, they knew that all matter was made up of atoms, but what, if anything, made up the atoms themselves? They knew that large batteries could make electric sparks jump through air. Why did that happen? They had seen that sparks could jump across a glass tube from which all the air had been removed. How could electricity pass through a vacuum? They also began to ask themselves about things they had previously taken for granted – for example, how did light travel through space?

ABOVE: *Every element has its own characteristic spectrum of coloured light. These are the colours emitted by the element helium.*

INTO THE ATOM

By the beginning of the twentieth century, scientists had settled a long-running debate about whether or not atoms – the fundamental building blocks of all things – existed. They did. All the chemical elements were made up of atoms, which had different properties depending on the element. In the space of a few years towards the end of the previous century a lot had been discovered about the nature of the atom. Scientists could work out the size of atoms in a particular chemical, and they knew they combined to make molecules. However, they still knew very little about what went on inside an atom.

Some tantalising clues came from a new science called spectroscopy, which studied the colours within visible light, and the different colours of light emitted by atoms of various elements. For example, a beam of light entering a glass prism undergoes a slight change in speed and direction, which causes the light to refract, or split, into a range of colours called a spectrum. The same thing happens when light passes through other mediums; a rainbow is the effect of sunlight being refracted through raindrops. Each colour in the spectrum has a different wavelength. Violet light has the shortest wavelength and red light has the longest.

Scientists noticed that under certain conditions, the atoms of chemical elements emit a characteristic set of coloured light as well. The appearance of particular colours suggested that a substance contained a particular element. For example, adding a chemical containing sodium into a gas flame makes the flame turn a distinctive orange colour. Spectroscopy was a useful way of analysing substances to find out what they were made of. The element helium was first discovered not on Earth but in the Sun, when its characteristic spectrum was detected in sunlight.

Remember

REFRACTION is when a ray of light changes direction as it passes from one medium to another — for example, from air to glass.

WAVELENGTH is the length of one complete wave cycle.

FREQUENCY is the number of complete waves made in one second; it is measured in Hertz (Hz).

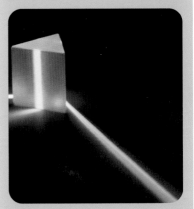

ABOVE: *When a ray of light passes through a prism, it is bent, or refracted, into the different colours of the spectrum.*

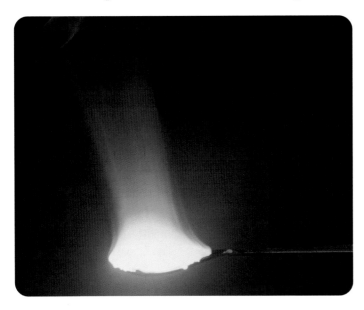

LEFT: *Scientists discovered that sodium burns with an orange light, and this way they were able to identify the element in different substances.*

Fact

ELECTROMAGNETIC WAVES

Today, some of the most important technical developments of James Clerk Maxwell's theory of electromagnetism are radio, television and radar. In Germany in 1884 Heinrich Hertz (1857-94) succeeded in generating electromagnetic waves using electric currents. He detected the waves when they caused a spark to jump out in a second electric circuit. Other scientists developed these experiments further and showed that radio waves could be sent as signals across oceans and even continents as a means of communication. By the 1920s, radio stations were broadcasting to audiences who now had radios in their own homes.

ABOVE: *Early radios, like this one from the 1920s, used Maxwell's theory of electromagnetism. An antenna picks up radio signals and sends them down the wire in the form of an electric current. There is another wire in the headphones that is caused to vibrate by the current, producing sound.*

LIGHT IS A WAVE

But how did atoms emit light? For many years, scientists had argued about whether light was a stream of particles or a wave. Experiments supported both ideas, but neither could explain all the behaviour of light. In the nineteenth century, James Clerk Maxwell, one of the leading British physicists of the time, developed the theory of electromagnetism, and used it to prove that light was, in fact, a wave. Electromagnetism is the combining of electric and magnetic fields (the areas around electric and magnetised bodies where a charge can be felt). Maxwell noticed the relationship between the two fields and realised that they were not independent phenomena, but that they depended on each other: an electric field produces a changing magnetic field, which in turn creates a changing electric field and so on. Energy is exchanged back and forth between the two fields, causing waves to move through space. This explains how light moves. It travels by means of a combination of electric and magnetic fields moving in step with each other. It is a kind of electromagnetic wave.

But if light is a wave, does that mean it needs a special material to travel through? A water wave travels through water, and needs the water to do so. So when light travels to Earth from the Sun, does this mean that space is filled with a special material that 'carries' the light waves? Physicists at the time thought this must be the case, and they called this material 'ether'.

Of course, no one could see ether, so scientists set about trying to prove it existed. In the 1880s in the United States, Albert Michelson (1852–1931) and Edward Morley (1838–1923) measured the speed of light at different times of the year to see if they could detect the effect of the ether's movement on light. Michelson and Morley found no difference in their measurements of the speed of light. This suggested that there was no such thing as ether. If that was the

Key People

James Clerk Maxwell (1831–79) was the British physicist who developed the theory of electromagnetism. In it he stated that the electromagnetic field is all around us. It is made up of the electric field, created by stationary charges, and the magnetic field, created by moving charges, each of which caused changes in the other. This was a turning-point in understanding the nature of light, which scientists had been speculating about for many years. Light moved through the electromagnetic field as a wave. Maxwell also predicted that there would be other, invisible, electromagnetic waves. These are what we now call the electromagnetic spectrum.

case, then light waves were not carried by anything at all – there was nothing in space that conducted sunlight to Earth. Light waves travelled in a vacuum and always travelled at the same speed.

The Michelson and Morley experiment became a landmark 'null result' in physics. (A 'null result' means that an experiment unquestionably proves a

BELOW: Albert Michelson who, together with Edward Morley, conducted a famous experiment to prove that ether existed. They discovered that it didn't!

Fact

THE ELECTROMAGNETIC SPECTRUM

The electromagnetic spectrum is the range of different kinds of waves that travel through space. They each come from different sources, and have different frequencies and wavelengths. However, all the wave types in the electromagnetic spectrum carry energy from one place to another. What we now know as 'visible light' (ordinary light) is just a very tiny part of the electromagnetic spectrum. James Clerk Maxwell predicted that there were many other types of electromagnetic waves, but it was some years before scientists discovered these. Now we know that they are:

★ GAMMA RAYS: dangerous, extremely high energy, short-wavelength radiation, capable of penetrating matter and causing much destruction.

BELOW: The types of radiation in the electro-magnetic spectrum all carry energy from one place to another. The wavelengths get longer as you move along the spectrum.

★ X-RAYS: bursts of high-energy electrons and ions capable of changing whatever they hit; not quite as penetrating or destructive as gamma rays.

★ ULTRAVIOLET RAYS: invisible radiation of a wavelength that causes certain materials to glow, or fluoresce.

★ VISIBLE LIGHT: electromagnetic wavelengths visible to humans and animals.

★ INFRARED RAYS: long-wavelength radiation that causes molecules to vibrate; detected as heat waves.

★ MICROWAVES: longer-wavelength radiation that causes a quicker and more intense heating of materials than infrared waves; also used in communication.

★ RADIO WAVES: the longest-wavelength radiation, capable of carrying audible and visual signals; prolonged exposure causes tissue damage at extremely low wavelengths and frequencies.

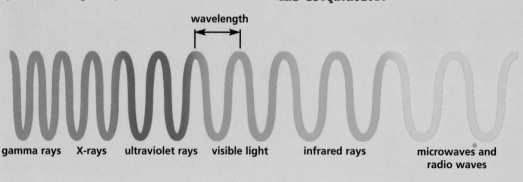

wavelength

gamma rays   X-rays   ultraviolet rays   visible light   infrared rays   microwaves and radio waves

theory wrong.) Now that scientists knew for sure that ether did not exist, they could start to consider other theories about light, physics and the Universe as a whole. The negative discovery sparked a revolution among scientific minds. Perhaps the great thinkers needed to reconsider other long-held beliefs and explore new aspects of their science.

This was an area of physics by which scientists were fascinated – and confused – during the period in which Einstein was growing up. By the time he settled into married life and his job at the patent office, however, Einstein was starting to think about light in quite a different way from most of the other scientists of the time.

X-RAYS, RADIOACTIVITY AND ELECTRONS

Light and electricity are important features of matter. But if matter is made up of atoms, how do the structure of the atom, light and electricity all fit together? Important clues came from three discoveries that took place in three years: X-rays, radioactivity and the electron.

In 1895 in Germany, Wilhelm Röntgen discovered a mysterious type of radiation that could pass through solid objects. He noticed the rays when they travelled through paper to blacken photographic film. Because he did not know what they were, Röntgen called them X-rays. Doctors quickly discovered that another feature of X-rays was that they could penetrate skin

BELOW: *X-rays can be used by doctors to see if bones are broken. The rays can pass through soft tissue, but are absorbed by hard material like bone, so an outline of the bone is formed on photographic paper.*

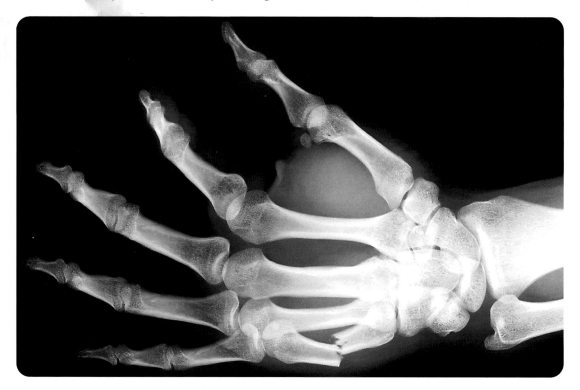

ABOVE: *Marie Curie continued the work begun by Henri Becquerel on radioactivity, and discovered more radioactive elements. She shared the Nobel Prize with Becquerel in 1903.*

and muscle but could not pass through bone, and so they were used for checking to see if bones were broken in patients. This is possible because their short wavelength means that most of the rays can pass through softer tissue to reach the photographic film, but when X-rays hit harder material like bone, more of them are absorbed. This is why X-ray photographs are 'negatives' – that is, the darker patches are where more X-rays have reached the other side and blackened the photographic paper.

The next discovery was made by Henri Becquerel (1852–1908) in Paris in 1896. He found that atoms of the element uranium emitted a radiation that, like X-rays, could blacken photographic plates wrapped in paper. This phenomenon is called radioactivity. Marie Curie (1867–1934) took up the study of radioactivity with enthusiasm and soon found other radioactive chemical elements – radium and polonium.

In England, J. J. Thomson (1856–1940) investigated the problems of electric currents passing through glass tubes. He discovered that he could change the direction of a beam of cathode rays (particles emitted through the negative electrode) using electric and magnetic fields. This meant that cathode rays were particles that had an electric charge. He had discovered the electron, the particle within an atom that has a negative electric charge.

What emerged from these discoveries was a radical set of theories that we now call quantum mechanics and relativity. Quantum mechanics is the laws of physics that apply on very small scales – not just what happens inside the nucleus of an atom, but the laws that govern what happens inside the particles that exist in the nucleus. It deals with the very smallest particles of matter in the Universe. Relativity – Albert Einstein's revolutionary theory – combined ideas about matter, time and space, and form the basis of our understanding of the Universe today.

BELOW: This is a Crookes tube, used by the British physicist Sir William Crookes to investigate cathode rays. Objects placed in the evacuated tube formed shadows on the glass, proving that the rays moved in straight lines. Later, J. J. Thomson used a cathode-ray tube similar to this in his own investigations, which led to the discovery of the electron.

Remember

RADIATION is simply a form of energy that travels through space, spreading out as it goes. All the wave types in the electromagnetic spectrum are forms of radiation.

RADIOACTIVITY is a type of radiation caused by the atomic breakdown of certain elements. For example, some forms of uranium are radioactive. They emit dangerous, invisible particles or rays.

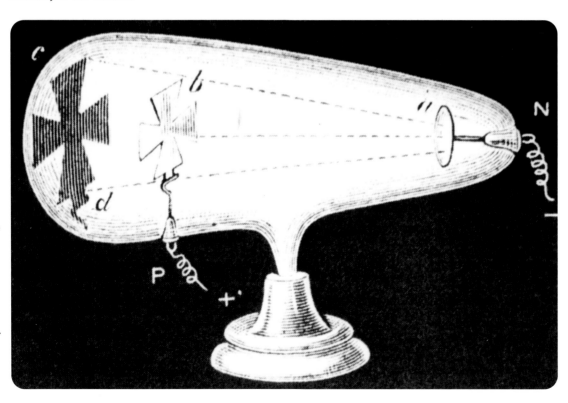

CHAPTER THREE

'When you are courting a nice girl an hour seems like a second. When you sit on a red-hot cinder a second seems like an hour. That's relativity.' **ALBERT EINSTEIN**

The Special Theory of Relativity

EINSTEIN, SPENDING HIS DAYS WORKING AT THE PATENT OFFICE, WAS fascinated by the questions surrounding the nature and speed of light. He began formulating some questions of his own and looking for the answers. In his spare time he wrote lots of papers outlining his ideas, and in 1905 these finally earned him his doctorate from the University of Zürich. This was a busy year for Einstein – he published three of his papers in 1905. One of these described what he called the 'Special Theory of Relativity', which made several predictions about the nature of light, time, mass and motion. It sent shockwaves through the scientific world!

ABOVE: Einstein was only 26 years old when he published his paper on the Special Theory of Relativity in 1905.

WHAT IS SPECIAL RELATIVITY?

When formulating Special Relativity, Einstein worked on two assumptions. The first was that there is no such thing as absolute rest; that is, there is no way of telling whether something is at rest or is moving steadily in one direction. All motion or rest is *relative* to other objects. Think of yourself standing very still. In relation to the Earth you are not moving at all. However, in relation to the Sun you are moving very rapidly, because the Earth is moving round the Sun. The second assumption Einstein made was that the speed of light is constant to any observer, whether they are moving or at rest.

Einstein discovered that in order for any observer to measure the same speed for a beam of light, time and space could not be uniform in the way that people thought they were, that is, the same for everyone no matter where they were or how fast they were moving: time would need to flow differently for each observer and space would sometimes have to contract. Special Theory predicts several things. The most important of these are: the mass of a body is equivalent to its energy (the famous $E=mc^2$ equation); the mass of a body increases as its speed increases; moving bodies get shorter; moving clocks run more slowly than stationary clocks. So, imagine someone watching, say, a rocket, travelling at almost the speed of light. As the rocket flashes by, the viewer would observe that the rocket's length had become shorter, its mass had increased, and any clock on the rocket had slowed down. This might sound like science fiction, but these predictions that Einstein made were later proved to be true.

TIME DILATION

The phenomenon of the clock running more slowly is called time dilation.

Picture someone facing a mirror. They flick on a torch and measure how long it takes for the light to travel from the torch to the mirror and back.

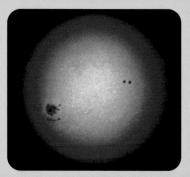

Fact

THE SPEED OF LIGHT
Light travels at about 300,000 kilometres per second. Light from the Sun takes about eight minutes to reach to Earth, a distance of 149 million kilometres. By the laws of relativity, nothing can travel faster than the speed of light. It is a kind of universal speed limit!

ABOVE: *Our planet can sustain life because light from the Sun reaches us in eight minutes. Light from other, more distant stars, can take thousands of years to reach Earth.*

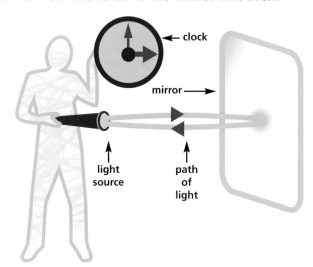

LEFT: *A scientist measures the speed of light by timing how long it takes for a beam of light to travel a certain distance, bounce off a mirror, and return to the source.*

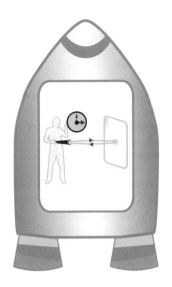

ABOVE: *Light's velocity is always the same, whether or not the person measuring it is moving. A person measuring the speed of light while aboard a moving spacecraft will end up with the same measurement as a person on Earth.*

Fact

PROVING THE
CLOCK PARADOX
For a rocket travelling
very fast, an outside
observer would see that
a clock on the rocket
has slowed down. Strange
though this seems, it
has been observed to
happen. Some subatomic
particles have a short
life. They change into
other particles after a
certain amount of time.
Experiments to measure
the lifetime of these
particles showed that
the lifetimes were
longer if they were
travelling very fast.
To an outside observer,
time had slowed down
for these particles.

Now imagine that exactly the same experiment takes place in a rocket travelling at a speed very close to the speed of light. For someone on the rocket, the time taken for the light to travel to the mirror and back is the same as it was in the first experiment. However, someone looking at the rocket as it flashes by will see something quite different.

A person viewing the experiment on the rocket from the Earth still sees the light travel to and from the mirror. However, the person in the rocket has moved in the time taken by the light beam to leave the torch, hit the mirror and return. To the observer outside the rocket, the light has travelled a longer path, so he or she will measure a longer time for the light beam to make its journey. The clocks on the rocket run slow compared to his own clock.

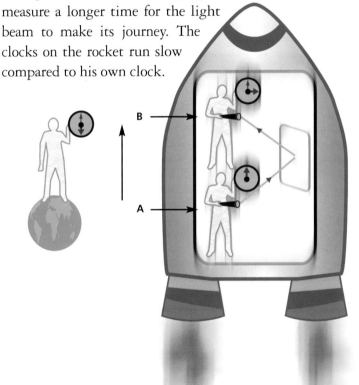

ABOVE: *While the speed of light is the same whether or not the observer is moving, the apparent passage of time differs. A clock held by a person on Earth (left) will experience a longer passage of time because of time dilation than a clock held by a person speeding from point A to point B through outer space. In this example, the person on Earth may think 30 seconds have passed, but the person in the spacecraft may think 15 seconds have passed. In reality, an astronaut aboard the International Space Station for a year will be about four seconds younger than if he or she had stayed on Earth for that year.*

RELATIVE MOTION

To understand the concept of relative motion, we need to look at another example.

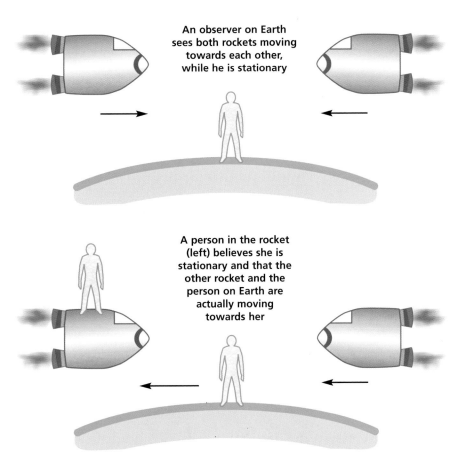

An observer on Earth sees both rockets moving towards each other, while he is stationary

A person in the rocket (left) believes she is stationary and that the other rocket and the person on Earth are actually moving towards her

Two people are in rockets, travelling towards each other at different speeds. An observer on the ground sees that both people are moving. However, the person in each of the rockets thinks that they are stationary and that in fact it is the other person that is moving towards them at a certain speed. (If they looked out of the window, they would also think that the observer on the ground was moving.) So, whether an object is perceived to be in motion or at rest depends on the observer – motion is *relative*.

The length of an object in motion is also relative to the observer. To the person in the rocket, its length remains unchanged. However, to the observer on the ground, the length of the rocket will contract (get smaller), the faster it travels. As the rocket approaches the speed of light, it appears to get smaller and smaller. If it could travel faster than the speed of light, its measured length would shrink to nothing. This is because the rocket would be moving faster than the light travelling back to the observer, so they would not be able to see it.

Fact

HOW FAR AWAY IS THE MOON?

Scientists used the speed of light to measure the exact distance to the Moon. When astronauts landed on the Moon in 1969, they left a mirror there. Back on Earth, a beam of light from a laser was directed at the mirror. The distance was worked out by measuring the time it took for the light to travel to the Moon, be reflected off the mirror, and bounce back to Earth again. Because the Moon travels round the Earth in an elliptical orbit (a slightly elongated rather than a perfect circle), the distance between the two bodies changes and therefore the time taken for the light to return to Earth is slightly different. At its closest, though, the Moon is 356,400 km away.

RIGHT: *These lasers are used to measure the distance from the Earth to objects in space. The laser on the left is measuring the distance to the Moon; the upright laser on the right is measuring the distance to satellites.*

EINSTEIN'S EQUATION: E=MC²

One of the most famous predictions Einstein made in 1905 was the equation $E = mc^2$, where E is energy, m is mass and c is the speed of light. Put simply, the equation means that energy and mass are different forms of the same thing.

If a person gets into a car and drives off, the car picks up speed when the accelerator is pressed. What is happening is that the engine and the transmission convert the chemical energy in the petrol into kinetic energy (the energy a body has because of its motion) of the moving car. The kinetic energy of the car depends on its mass and its speed. When you burn something – petrol in a motor-car engine for example – and heat is produced, some mass has been turned into energy.

Now, imagine a person in a spaceship fires the rocket engines to increase its speed. The mass of the fuel is converted into energy. However, the energy

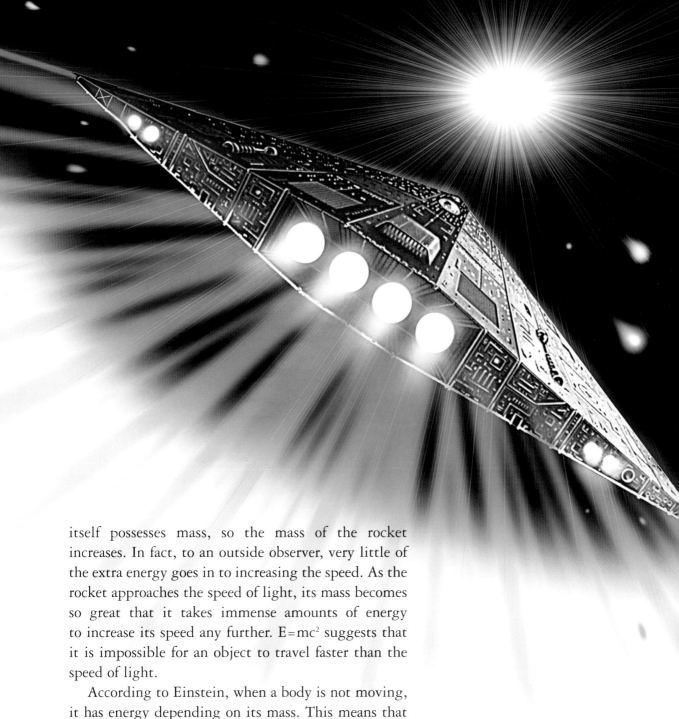

itself possesses mass, so the mass of the rocket increases. In fact, to an outside observer, very little of the extra energy goes in to increasing the speed. As the rocket approaches the speed of light, its mass becomes so great that it takes immense amounts of energy to increase its speed any further. $E = mc^2$ suggests that it is impossible for an object to travel faster than the speed of light.

According to Einstein, when a body is not moving, it has energy depending on its mass. This means that mass can be converted into energy and vice versa. The conversion factor is the speed of light squared. It takes very little mass to make a lot of energy – mass is a very concentrated form of energy.

On an everyday level, changes in mass are so small they cannot easily be detected. However, in processes involving large amounts of energy, the change in mass becomes more obvious. An example of this is when a

ABOVE: *As a spaceship approaches the speed of light, more and more energy is needed for acceleration, but as Einstein's equation suggested that energy and mass are the same thing, eventually its mass will become so great that it cannot accelerate further. The spaceship will not be able to travel faster than the speed of light.*

Fact

THE PHOTOELECTRIC EFFECT

In the same year that he published his Special Theory of Relativity, Einstein also released another paper, outlining his theories on another aspect of physics that scientists had been puzzling over. This was what he called the 'photoelectric effect'. During experiments, physicists had noticed that when light falls on a metal plate, sometimes electric charges are released from that plate. This only happens with light of certain wavelengths, though (these can be distinguished by the colour of the light). Einstein realised that the light hits the plate in a series of 'packets', which he called 'quanta'. The energy of these packets depends on the type of light — ultraviolet light has a high energy, but red light has low energy. A packet of light has to have a certain amount of energy to force an atom to absorb it and release an electron — the electric charge scientists had seen. Einstein received the Nobel Prize for his explanation of the photoelectric effect.

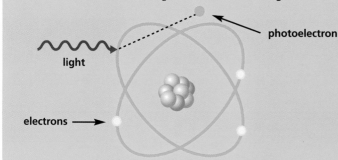

light

photoelectron

electrons ⟶

LEFT: Einstein explained the photoelectric effect by suggesting that individual particles (or quanta) of light penetrated the metal and knocked electrons free from atoms.

uranium nucleus splits in two, a process called nuclear fission. After the uranium nucleus splits, the different particles produced have less mass than the original uranium nucleus. This is because some of the mass has been released as energy. This energy provides the heat in a nuclear power station or the explosion for a nuclear weapon. This is an example of $E=mc^2$.

RIGHT: Nuclear power stations like this one in Gloucestershire actually use Einstein's prediction about mass and energy ($E=mc^2$). They use a process called nuclear fission, in which some of the mass of atomic nuclei is converted into energy, which generates heat.

LEFT: Although Einstein's Special Theory of Relativity explained much about the way the Universe might work, he knew that a key element was missing from his ideas – gravity.

WHATEVER NEXT?

The Special Theory of Relativity and $E = mc^2$ rocked the scientific world in 1905. The ideas were revolutionary and there was no way of proving they were accurate at the time. All Einstein had done was present a new system of looking at time, speed, motion and matter. No one had thought of things in this way before, and physicists began to question many preconceptions they had held about the Universe. If they accepted Einstein's basic assumptions, then his theories made a lot of sense. He became celebrated as a genius in scientific fields. Einstein did not care about this, though. He knew that although he had set the wheels in motion for a radical rethinking of the laws of the Universe, the theories were not perfect. There were other factors that needed to be brought into play – the most important of these was gravity.

Fact

A SUMMARY OF SPECIAL RELATIVITY

★ TIME IS RELATIVE: time is measured differently by different observers. Time 'slows down' at speeds approaching the speed of light.

★ SPACE IS RELATIVE: space is measured differently by different observers. A path of light seems longer to a stationary observer if he or she is observing the light travelling at very high speeds.

★ ENERGY AND MASS ARE DIFFERENT FORMS OF THE SAME THING: mass can be converted into energy and energy can be converted into mass. All matter is a form of energy and therefore cannot be created or destroyed; it can only change form.

CHAPTER FOUR

'If my theory of relativity is proven correct, Germany will claim me as a German and France will declare that I am a citizen of the world. Should my theory prove untrue, France will say that I am a German and Germany will declare that I am a Jew.' ALBERT EINSTEIN, 1929

The General Theory of Relativity

ABOVE: *We can see the effect of gravity on Earth by looking at the tides. The Moon pulls on the Earth because of gravity, so the water on Earth is also pulled, causing a kind of 'bulge' and creating tides.*

Remember

GRAVITY is the force acting between any two masses or bodies — the attraction that exists between all objects.

IN 1908 EINSTEIN FINALLY GOT A JOB AS A lecturer, at the University of Bern, but he moved on quickly when offered the post of Professor of Physics at the University of Zürich the following year. By 1914 he had moved back to his native Germany to take up an even more eminent position at the University of Berlin. He was, by this time, highly regarded in his field – one of the leading scientific thinkers of the time. But his most radical work was yet to come. In 1915, as the First World War raged, Einstein released another paper, building on the earlier one. He called it the General Theory of Relativity, or GTR, and in it he considered gravity.

NEWTON'S THEORY OF GRAVITY

Isaac Newton had developed a theory of gravity in 1687. In it, he explained that any two bodies were attracted to each other with a force that depended on the masses of the bodies involved and the distance between them. In this way, his force – gravity –

accounted for both the motion of the Moon and an apple falling from a tree, for example. The Earth pulls on the Moon and on the apple. At the same time, the Moon and the apple each attract the Earth.

We are only really aware of the gravitational pull of the Earth itself, especially when we fall over or drop something heavy. But we can also see the effects of the gravitational pull of the Sun and Moon. An example of this is the tides, which are caused by the gravitational pull of the Moon on the Earth.

Although he described the effects of gravity very accurately, Newton did not actually explain how it worked. How exactly did the Earth attract nearby objects towards its centre? In fact this was the subject of a fierce debate in the late seventeenth century.

Again Einstein had a remarkable insight that dealt with this problem. He explained it: 'For an observer falling freely from the roof of a house there exists – at least in his immediate surroundings – no gravitational field.'

What he had observed was that when something is dropped, while it is falling it seems to the body that no force acts on it. A force speeds up, slows down, or changes the direction of an object. In free fall, a body has reached terminal velocity – it has accelerated to a point where it has stopped speeding up and instead travels at that constant speed and in a straight line. So when a body is in free fall it seems as though there is no force acting on it. In the case of Einstein's person falling from the roof, the forces of gravity and air resistance balance each other. In a vacuum, like space, there is not even air resistance. A floating object that is stationary has no net force acting on it because the forces are balanced.

From this observation, Einstein explained how mass affected the properties of space. Massive objects like

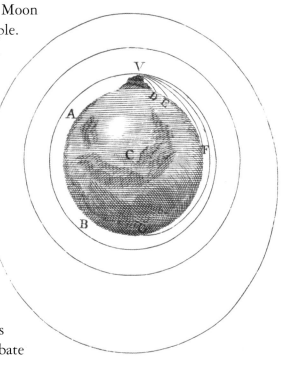

ABOVE: *This is one of Newton's drawings to describe gravity. It shows a map of the Earth and the paths of an object orbiting it, which has been launched from a high mountain. At low speeds (D, E, F and G), the object only travels short distances before it hits Earth because of gravity. At high speeds, it escapes gravity and orbits the Earth (A, B). At even greater speeds the object would move in an elliptical orbit further away – the outer two rings.*

Key People

Sir Isaac Newton (1642–1727) was an English scientist and mathematician whose experiments opened up a whole new world of discovery in the seventeenth century. In Einstein's time – 200 years later – the accepted laws that ruled the Universe and everything in it were still based on Newton's ideas. Newton was the first to suggest that a force he called 'gravity' existed in the Universe, and it was this that stopped, for example, the Moon falling into the Earth. He could not explain exactly what gravity was, but he devised a series of rules that showed how it worked. Newton also conducted experiments with light, and was the first to notice that white light could be split into different colours using a prism. He also built his own telescopes and used these to make observations of the stars and planets.

the Sun distort space so that small bodies nearby no longer travel in straight lines: the paths they followed are curved. More than two centuries after Newton had described and measured the effects of gravity, Einstein's General Theory of Relativity explained how it worked.

RIGHT: *The General Theory of Relativity replaced gravity with curved space-time. Massive objects like the Sun distort this space-time so that nearby objects do not move in straight lines, but rather are forced into curved paths.*

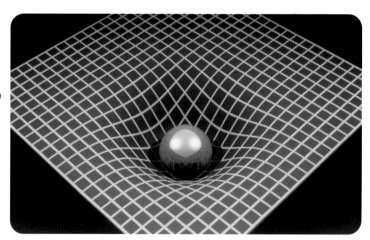

TESTING GENERAL RELATIVITY

An opportunity to test Einstein's new theory came very soon after the end of the First World War. In May 1919 there was a total eclipse of the Sun that would be observable in Africa and South America. During an eclipse, the Sun's light is blocked out, making stars visible during the day.

If Einstein's theory was correct, then light from distant stars passing near the Sun would travel in a curved path rather than a straight line. If scientists looked close to the edge of

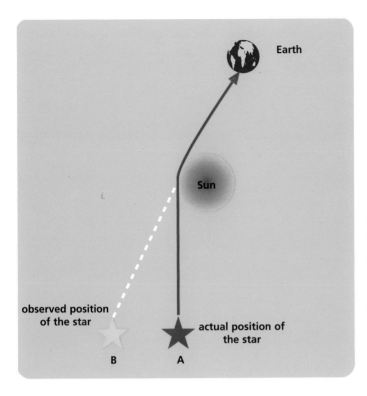

Earth

observed position
of the star

B

actual position of
the star

A

Sun

LEFT: Space-time curves space around large objects like the Sun, so that the light from a star that is really in position A (behind the Sun) appears as though it is at position B if viewed from the Earth.

Fact

WHAT IS FREE FALL?
'Free fall' is used to describe any object that is moving freely in a gravitational field, with no other forces acting on it, or when forces are balanced. Stars and planets are in free fall. So is our Moon and even the man-made satellites that orbit the Earth. When an astronaut goes into space, he feels 'weightless'. This is not because there is no gravitational force acting on him – there is, and it is not much less than the gravity felt on Earth. Astronauts feel 'weightless' because they are in free fall.

ABOVE: *Astronauts in space do not feel any forces acting on them – they are in free fall.*

the Sun's disc during the eclipse, they would see the light from a star that was actually behind the Sun if its light had indeed travelled in a curved path to Earth. If light from the star travelled in a straight line, it would not reach Earth and the star would not be visible during the eclipse. The 1919 eclipse was an opportunity for a very dramatic test of Einstein's new theory.

Several expeditions were mounted to observe the eclipse off West Africa and in Brazil. On Principe, an island off West Africa, Arthur Eddington measured the bending of light from one particular star. He found that Einstein's prediction was correct. The light was bent by a small fraction of one degree. This experiment was seen as a triumph for Einstein's General Theory of Relativity.

WHAT DID IT ALL MEAN?

If Einstein's General Theory of Relativity was correct – and early observations like the ones made by Eddington in 1919 suggested it was – then the Universe has to be seen not in three dimensions, but in four. The idea of a fourth dimension was not new.

Key People

Sir Arthur Eddington (1882–1944) was an English physicist, mathematician and astronomer. He was working at Cambridge University (where he remained for his whole career) when he first heard of Einstein's General Theory of Relativity. Radical as it was, the theory made sense to Eddington – it explained for the first time why heavenly bodies in orbit do not eventually crash into other bodies. He was one of Einstein's earliest supporters, and helped bring evidence of the theory's accuracy to the world when he observed the bending of a star's light by the Sun's gravitational field during the eclipse in 1919.

Scientists had thought of time as a kind of fourth dimension for centuries. In Newton's laws of physics there were three dimensions of space and one of time. Any event could be defined by where it happened (three co-ordinates) and when it happened (one co-ordinate). However, in Einstein's Universe, space and time combined to make up one four-dimensional entity, space-time. In this Universe, free fall is actually the natural state for all bodies – not rest or constant speed. Bodies like the Earth are kept in orbit around the Sun by the curvature of space-time.

When the results of Eddington's observations during the eclipse were reported in November 1919 there was tremendous popular interest. The reports appeared in newspapers around the world. The *New York Times* carried the headline 'Lights all askew in the heavens. Einstein theory triumphs.' In England, the *Times* read 'Revolution in science. New theory of the Universe. Newtonian ideas overthrown.'

The reports in the newspapers about the tests of Einstein's General Theory of Relativity were the beginnings of wide popular interest in Einstein and his ideas. He became one of the great scientific heroes of the age. In 1921, he was awarded the Nobel Prize for Physics – surprisingly for his explanation of the photoelectric effect rather than his theories of relativity. Einstein had divorced Mileva two years previously, and almost immediately remarried – this time to his second cousin, Elsa Löwenthal. When he received the money from the Nobel Prize, Einstein gave it all to Mileva. With a mass of unruly hair and a strange preference for not wearing socks, Einstein lived up to the image of the scientist as an eccentric person only interested in complicated ideas.

EINSTEIN IN THE INTERWAR YEARS

Einstein had been living in Germany throughout the First World War. He was a pacifist – he did not agree with war and thought there were better ways to solve differences. During the First World War he had even signed a petition protesting against the war, which was sent to the ruler of Germany, Kaiser Wilhelm. This was a brave thing to do, as he could have lost his position at the University. After the country was defeated it was forced to make reparations – giving land and money to the countries that had won the war. Times were hard in Germany for many years. Many people were unemployed and there was great social unrest. By the early 1930s this had given rise to several new political parties, including the National Socialist Party and the German Communist Party. Germany was already on the road to the Second World War.

In 1932 Einstein left Berlin to visit the Institute for Advanced Study at the University of Princeton in the United States. Einstein intended to return to Germany, but he never did so.

In 1933 the National Socialist Party, led by Hitler, came to power in Germany. One consequence of this was that Jewish people could no longer be civil servants. Einstein was Jewish. As university posts were in the civil service, many prominent scientists lost their jobs.

Another result of this anti-Jewish sentiment was that some German physicists argued that relativity and several other new ideas about physics that had been developed in the previous few years were suspect theories because many of their authors were Jewish. All this turmoil meant that Einstein had little to gain by returning to Germany. He would remain in the United States for the rest of his life.

ABOVE: *Einstein with his second wife, Elsa Löwenthal, photographed in 1921, the year Einstein received the Nobel Prize for his explanation of the photoelectric effect.*

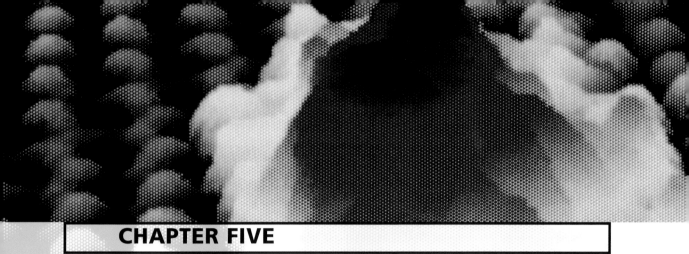

CHAPTER FIVE

'The unleashed power of the atom has changed everything save our modes of thinking and we thus drift toward unparalleled catastrophe.' **ALBERT EINSTEIN, 1946**

Relativity and Nuclear Power

ABOVE: *Today, scientists can actually 'see' atoms using a special microscope called a scanning-tunnelling microscope. The yellow, red and brown parts here are atoms of gold, and they measure about 1.5 nanometres (billionths of a metre) at the base.*

THE GENERAL THEORY OF RELATIVITY explained the laws that governed massive bodies in space, like the stars and the planets. It also partly explained the behaviour of the tiniest pieces of matter known at the time – subatomic particles. The study of physics that applies to very small scales like this became known as quantum mechanics.

INSIDE THE NUCLEUS

During the 1920s, with the development of quantum mechanics, more and more details of the structure of the atom became clear. Between 1911 and 1913, the physicists Ernest Rutherford (1871–1937) and Niels Bohr (1885–1962) showed that the atom had a central core, the nucleus, which contained a positive electric charge and most of the mass of the atom. Around this nucleus travelled the negatively charged electrons in an arrangement of orbits. Throughout the 1920s, scientists learned even more about the behaviour of these electrons, but the greatest mystery remained: what went on inside the nucleus?

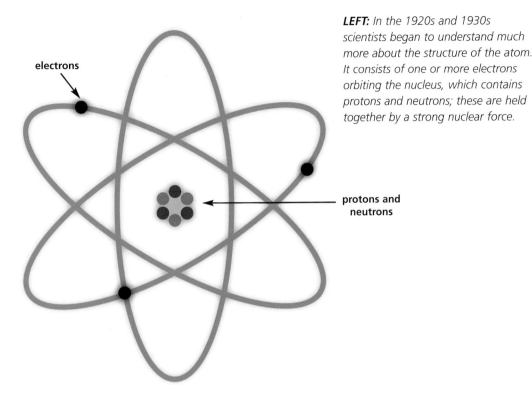

electrons

protons and
neutrons

LEFT: In the 1920s and 1930s scientists began to understand much more about the structure of the atom. It consists of one or more electrons orbiting the nucleus, which contains protons and neutrons; these are held together by a strong nuclear force.

Since Rutherford had first suggested the existence of the nucleus in 1911, it was clear that this central core had a positive electric charge to balance the negative electric charges of the electrons orbiting around it. Rutherford suggested that there was a unit of positive charge, the proton, present in all nuclei. But what else was there? The 1930s saw a flood of answers. So much so that a new field of science – nuclear physics – came into being. A series of discoveries in the early 1930s helped physicists understand the detailed structure of the nucleus.

In 1932, the English scientist James Chadwick (1891–1974) discovered the neutron. This was a particle that also existed in the nucleus of an atom. It had about the same mass as the proton but it was neutral – it had no electric charge. In Germany, Werner Heisenberg (1901–76) argued that apart from their electrical charges, protons and neutrons were very similar, and that there was another force, which he called the 'strong force' that held these particles in the nucleus.

THE DISCOVERY OF NUCLEAR FISSION

Another development for nuclear physics was particle accelerators. These huge machines, which could make nuclear particles travel at very high speeds, meant that scientists could do many more experiments. It was now possible to measure the energy involved in nuclear reactions very accurately, and to compare this with the masses of the particles involved.

Using a particle accelerator, a stream of neutrons was used as a projectile to 'shoot' at a target nucleus. By doing this, scientists hoped to create atoms of new elements that

ABOVE: *Today's particle accelerators are huge, hi-tech machines that can force collisions between subatomic particles at very high speeds. The blue light here is beams of electrons; the pink is beams of positrons.*

BELOW: *Otto Hahn and Lise Meitner had worked together in Berlin for nearly 30 years before they started to investigate nuclear fission. Meitner in particular faced much prejudice – not only because she was a woman working in a field dominated by men, but also, by the 1930s, because she was a Jew.*

were unknown on Earth. One man who tried this technique was the Italian physicist Enrico Fermi (1901–54). He wanted to create atoms of a new element by getting some of the neutrons to 'stick' to the nuclei of the heaviest chemical element then known, uranium. Similar experiments were undertaken in Germany in 1938 by Otto Hahn (1879–1968) and Fritz Strassmann (1902–80). All of them found a problem. Rather than creating a completely new element, as they had expected, they found that bombarding uranium nuclei with neutrons actually created atoms of the element barium. A barium nucleus has roughly half the mass of a uranium nucleus.

Hahn sent the results of these experiments to a former colleague, Lise Meitner (1878–1968), who was working in Sweden. Meitner had worked with Hahn in Berlin for many years. Although she was Jewish, she had kept her position in Berlin because she was Austrian. The situation for Jews in Germany soon worsened, however, and in 1938 Meitner lost her job and left the country to continue her research in Sweden.

Meitner discussed Hahn's curious results with her nephew Otto Frisch (1904–79). Between them they determined what had happened to the uranium during the experiment. Instead of 'sticking' to the uranium nucleus and changing its properties to form atoms of a new element, the incoming neutron had actually split the uranium nucleus. The barium that Hahn and Strassmann had found was amongst the debris that was created. They called this process 'fission'. The most important observation they made was that when a uranium nucleus underwent fission, energy was released. During the process some of the mass of the nucleus was turned into energy. Einstein was right! Mass and energy were two forms of the same thing. Such experiments proved the equation $E = mc^2$ and gave even more strength to Einstein's theories of relativity.

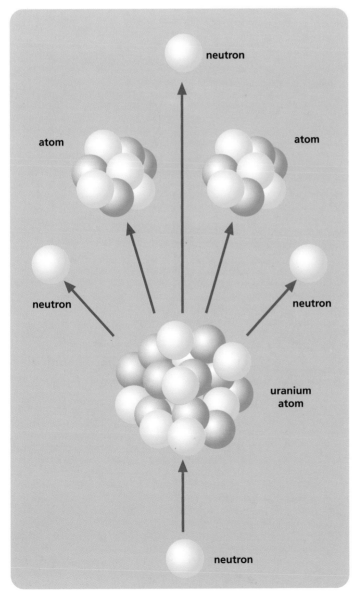

LEFT: *In the process of nuclear fission, the nucleus of a uranium atom is bombarded with neutrons. The neutron splits the atom into two lighter atoms (these might be atoms of several elements) and releases two or three other neutrons. These new neutrons are energy that has been converted from some of the mass of the original atom. Einstein's equation $E = mc^2$ is correct!*

EINSTEIN'S FEARS

World war was looming and refugees had already left Germany and Austria, among them Einstein and Meitner. Once they arrived in Britain and the United States, many of these refugee scientists were not allowed to work on wartime research projects such as radar because they were considered to be 'enemy aliens'. Instead, they turned their attentions to developing nuclear fission. They believed that if the energy released by uranium nuclei during fission could be harnessed, they could use it to make weapons more powerful than any that existed at the time.

In August 1939, Einstein wrote a letter to the president of the United States, Franklin D. Roosevelt. In it, he warned the president just how powerful a weapon using nuclear fission might be. He also warned that although many of Germany's best scientists had fled the country, there were others who might still be trying to develop a nuclear weapon.

The problem physicists found in developing this nuclear weapon was that ordinary uranium was not a good material for studies of nuclear fission. It was the isotope uranium 235 – a slightly different atom of uranium – in which fission worked most efficiently. Uranium 235 is very rare, so when uranium was bombarded with neutrons, the chances of a neutron hitting a uranium 235 nucleus were very small. Many scientists lost interest.

Fact

EINSTEIN'S LETTER

In August 1939, Einstein wrote to President Roosevelt to express his concerns about the recent developments in nuclear fission:

'*Some recent work ... leads me to expect that the element uranium may be turned into a new and important source of energy in the immediate future. Certain aspects of the situation which has arisen seem to call for watchfulness and, if necessary, quick action on the part of the Administration {the US government}....*

This new phenomenon would also lead to the construction of bombs, and it is conceivable – though much less certain – that extremely powerful bombs of a new type may be constructed. A single bomb of this type, carried by boat and exploded in a port, might very well destroy the whole port together with some of the surrounding territory.'

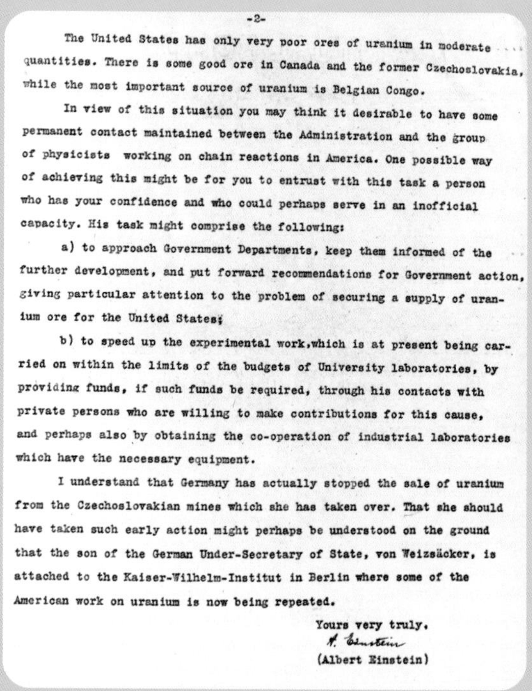

~2~

The United States has only very poor ores of uranium in moderate quantities. There is some good ore in Canada and the former Czechoslovakia, while the most important source of uranium is Belgian Congo.

In view of this situation you may think it desirable to have some permanent contact maintained between the Administration and the group of physicists working on chain reactions in America. One possible way of achieving this might be for you to entrust with this task a person who has your confidence and who could perhaps serve in an inofficial capacity. His task might comprise the following:

a) to approach Government Departments, keep them informed of the further development, and put forward recommendations for Government action, giving particular attention to the problem of securing a supply of uranium ore for the United States;

b) to speed up the experimental work, which is at present being carried on within the limits of the budgets of University laboratories, by providing funds, if such funds be required, through his contacts with private persons who are willing to make contributions for this cause, and perhaps also by obtaining the co-operation of industrial laboratories which have the necessary equipment.

I understand that Germany has actually stopped the sale of uranium from the Czechoslovakian mines which she has taken over. That she should have taken such early action might perhaps be understood on the ground that the son of the German Under-Secretary of State, von Weizsäcker, is attached to the Kaiser-Wilhelm-Institut in Berlin where some of the American work on uranium is now being repeated.

Yours very truly,

A. Einstein

(Albert Einstein)

ABOVE: *Part of Einstein's letter to US President Franklin D. Roosevelt.*

THE MANHATTAN PROJECT

Two physicists who continued to search for a way of making a nuclear weapon were Frisch and his colleague Rudolf Peierls (1907–95). They were working in England, researching uranium isotopes (atoms of the same element but which have different numbers of neutrons and therefore different masses). Frisch and Peierls realised that if they could separate the isotope uranium 235 from ordinary uranium, they would be able to use the isotope more efficiently. While this would be difficult to do, only a few kilograms of uranium 235 would be required to make a weapon.

Further research was carried out in Britain. However, it soon became clear that the scientific and industrial effort was beyond the resources available in wartime Britain – and any new factory would be a target for German bombing. The USA entered the war in December 1941 and this opened up greater resources for scientists. Mindful of Einstein's warning that the Germans could well be developing their own nuclear weapons, the United States set up its own atomic bomb programme, the Manhattan Project. As an 'enemy alien' Einstein was not part of the Manhattan Project. Instead it was directed by General Leslie Groves (1896–1970) of the US army. The leading scientist was Robert Oppenheimer, who was in charge of a team of scientists and engineers that devised and built the first nuclear weapons. They followed two routes. One was to separate uranium 235

ABOVE: *This is a 'button' of uranium 235, the isotope of ordinary uranium that was found to be much more efficient in nuclear fission. It is used as a fuel in nuclear reactors and is very precious. This piece alone is worth more than £100,000!*

LEFT: *Three of the most famous theoretical physicists of the 1930s and 1940s: (left to right) Paul Dirac, Wolfgang Pauli and Rudolf Peierls. Dirac later predicted the existence of antimatter. Pauli studied the behaviour of electrons in atoms, and Peierls famously worked out how to separate uranium 235 so it could be used in a nuclear weapon.*

Key People

Robert Oppenheimer (1904–67) is known as the 'father of the atomic bomb'. The American physicist led the team of scientists that found a way of separating plutonium from uranium, and using it in nuclear fission. This was the key to creating atomic weapons. Oppenheimer became caught up in the excitement of creating something new, and rising to the challenge of developing a weapon that could help his country win the war. Later he was overawed by the massive power of the atomic bomb, and the huge number of lives it could claim. He later campaigned strongly for the control of nuclear weapons. He also opposed the development of the hydrogen bomb that the USA went on to make. He continued to research physics, but he also examined the moral dilemmas that scientists often face in situations like this.

BELOW: This is a coloured aerial view of the test site of the first atomic bomb, the result of the Manhattan Project. The 'Trinity' bomb was detonated in the Los Alamos desert. The dark patch is an area of glass, created by the intense heat of the explosion on the desert sand.

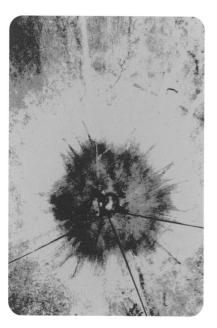

to use in a weapon, in the way that Frisch and Peierls had suggested (although these two scientists were not involved with the Manhattan Project either). The other was to manufacture another element, plutonium, by bombarding uranium with neutrons in a nuclear reactor. The advantage of this second method was that the isotope plutonium 239 could be used to make a nuclear weapon, but because it was a different chemical element it could be separated from the uranium by chemical methods relatively easily. Uranium isotopes can only be separated from each other by physical means, which makes it much more difficult.

After a huge scientific and industrial effort – involving billions of dollars at 1940s prices, and the work of hundreds of thousands of people – the first nuclear weapons were ready for use in the middle of 1945.

ATOMIC BOMBS

The war in Europe had ended shortly before, in May 1945. Although the Germans did have a programme to develop nuclear weapons, it had not advanced nearly as far as the British and Americans had feared. This was partly because the German authorities had not

HIROSHIMA AND NAGASAKI
Einstein's prediction
about the incredible
power of nuclear weapons
had been correct. When
the first atomic bomb
was dropped on Hiroshima
on 6 August 1945, 70,000
people were killed
instantly and the same
number injured. In
Nagasaki, three days
later, 40,000 were killed
immediately, and another
60,000 injured. Ten
square kilometres in
Hiroshima and eight
square kilometres in
Nagasaki were completely
destroyed. Even worse,
the radiation caused by
the bombs continued to
cause harm long after
the bombs were dropped,
and people continued to
suffer the effects.

ABOVE: *The atomic bomb blast over the Japanese city of Nagasaki in August 1945. The mushroom cloud rose over 18,000 metres into the air. More than 150,000 people were killed or injured directly from the blast, and thousands more suffered after-effects from the radiation.*

seen an atomic bomb as the highest priority during wartime. They had expected to win the Second World War quickly and so, even if nuclear weapons were possible, they would not be ready in time to influence the outcome of the war. Consequently, the Germans saw the possibilities of nuclear power and nuclear weapons as longer-term prospects to be pursued after the end of the war.

Even with the resources available in the United States, the first nuclear weapons were not ready by the end of the war in Europe. In July 1945 the USA tested its first nuclear weapon at Alamogordo in New Mexico. A few weeks later, the USA dropped two atomic bombs on the Japanese cities of Hiroshima and Nagasaki. Japan surrendered a few days later, ending the Second World War. It was clear to everyone, particularly the Russians, that the world had entered a new era — one in which weapons had reached levels of power and destruction that had been previously unimaginable.

CHAPTER SIX

'To raise new questions, new possibilities, to regard old problems from a new angle, requires creative imagination and marks real advance in science.' **ALBERT EINSTEIN**

Einstein's Legacy

EINSTEIN'S WORK ON RELATIVITY HAS LEFT TWO IMPORTANT LEGACIES. The first is that the General Theory of Relativity can be used to explore the size, shape and development of the Universe since the moments after the Big Bang – the origin of the Universe as it is generally accepted today. Experiments in high-energy physics are recreating the conditions that existed shortly after the Big Bang, so the General Theory of Relativity and quantum mechanics, the two areas to which Einstein made such important contributions, are becoming united. Relativity can be applied to the whole Universe and to the tiniest particles in it.

ABOVE: *The Crab nebula is what remains of a bright star that exploded in AD 1054 – Chinese astronomers witnessed and recorded the event. Right at the very centre is a pulsar – a spinning neutron star that emits pulses of radiation 30 times a second; most of the mass of neutron stars has been converted into energy, proving Einstein's equation E=mc².*

THE BIG BANG AND BLACK HOLES

During the 1920s and 1930s, astronomers and physicists investigated the problem of how stars produce the huge amounts of energy they do. Gradually it became clear that one of the main reactions taking place in a star was the fusion of hydrogen nuclei to make helium nuclei, releasing energy in the process. As with nuclear fission, this was an example of mass being converted into energy. So $E = mc^2$ does control the Universe!

In the 1960s a new set of problems arose. By this time, some physicists believed that the Universe as we know it had originated in what they called a 'Big Bang'. They had begun to think about what happened to a star when it reached the end of its life. Stars need energy to burn, but eventually the chemical processes within a star will not be able to generate enough energy to sustain its great mass and it will start to collapse. Perhaps it was possible for a star to collapse in on itself so much that light or matter could not escape from it. You would not be able to see these stars, they would just appear as black holes in space. Dead stars became known as black holes. But how could their existence be detected? In 1967 scientists discovered pulsars – stars that are very near the end of their lives. They have collapsed so far that they are only about 20 km across – absolutely tiny compared with stars at other stages of their lives. Pulsars can be detected only because they send out 'pulses' of energy. If a star can collapse to such a degree, it is likely that eventually it will collapse further, to a point that physicists call a singularity, where gravity is so great that it pulls everything into it and not even light can escape – a black hole.

Working on theories of this process, Roger Penrose (b. 1931) and Stephen Hawking (b. 1942) extended Einstein's General Theory of Relativity to envisage what happened very shortly after the Big Bang. What resulted was a combining of the General Theory of Relativity and quantum mechanics. In the extreme conditions of the Big Bang, matter did not exist as the atoms or molecules that we are familiar with today. What existed was a very dense 'soup' of quarks – the fundamental particles that came together to make protons and neutrons, which in turn form the atoms that we know.

EINSTEIN'S UNIFIED FIELD THEORY

Einstein's work on relativity had led him to believe that it must be possible to find one complete theory that would explain the working of the whole Universe and all physical phenomena. He called this a Unified Field Theory. One of his greatest inspirations came from James Clerk Maxwell and his theory of

Fact

WHAT WAS THE BIG BANG?
Scientists believe that the Big Bang happened somewhere between 10 and 20 billion years ago. In the Big Bang, all the matter and energy in the Universe was concentrated in a very hot, dense state. From this state, it 'exploded' and started to expand and cool down. As the Universe cooled, the fundamental particles that existed formed protons and neutrons, the building blocks of atomic nuclei. You can see from this theory that understanding the way the tiniest particles of matter work can help us understand how the largest thing we can imagine – the Universe – also works. Einstein's theories on relativity and quantum mechanics are the keys to this understanding.

ABOVE: *This diagram shows how the Universe might have looked shortly after the Big Bang, as matter started to form.*

Fact

BLACK HOLES

In 1967 Antony Hewish (b. 1924) and Jocelyn Bell (b. 1943) in England announced the discovery of pulsars. These were small stars about 20 km in diameter. They are very, very dense for their size. Because the matter is so concentrated, they are like one gigantic nucleus, hence their other name, neutron stars. With their discovery, the possibility of black holes was more likely. These are smaller than neutron stars and the effects of gravity are greater. For a time it was thought that nothing could escape from a black hole. Nearby matter, stars and gas would be sucked in and disappear. You would only be able to tell that a black hole was there by looking at the behaviour of other bodies nearby. Recently Stephen Hawking has suggested that in fact some information might be able to escape from black holes after all.

ABOVE: *Black holes are stars that have come to the end of their lives. They have completely collapsed in on themselves and gravity is so strong that even light cannot escape. Scientists can only tell that black holes exist because of the behaviour of other bodies near the black hole.*

Fact

NUCLEAR FUSION

Nuclear fusion works in the opposite way to nuclear fission. In fission, a nucleus is split; in fusion, two nuclei are 'fused' together and a different element is created. Energy is still released in the reaction and because of this, scientists realised they could use fusion, as well as fission, to create weapons; because the nuclei used in fusion are those of hydrogen atoms, these were called hydrogen bombs. Fusion happens naturally in the Sun, which is really a ball of energy caused by billions of simultaneous, continuous fusion reactions as hydrogen nuclei form helium atoms.

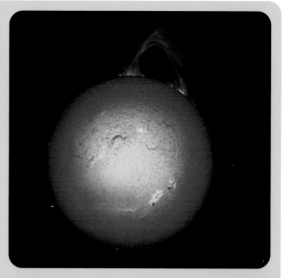

ABOVE: *Solar prominences like the one pictured are eruptions of hydrogen gas in the Sun. Hydrogen atoms fuse to form helium atoms.*

Remember

A NUCLEAR BOMB is any bomb that uses nuclear reactions to create massive and destructive amounts of energy.

AN ATOMIC BOMB is a bomb that uses nuclear fission to release energy; the elements used in atomic bombs are either uranium or plutonium.

A HYDROGEN BOMB is a bomb that uses nuclear fusion to release energy; the element used is hydrogen.

'Nothing that I can do will change the structure of the Universe. But maybe, by raising my voice I can help the greatest of all causes – goodwill among men and peace on earth.' **ALBERT EINSTEIN**

electromagnetism. Maxwell had taken two theories – one about electricity and another about magnetism – and united them. This was one of the outstanding achievements in science in the nineteenth century. Maxwell showed how light was a form of electromagnetic radiation, and predicted that other invisible electromagnetic waves were possible. This eventually led to the development of radio, television, radar and mobile phones – all things that we take for granted today. If Maxwell had united electricity and magnetism, would it be possible to add in other theories such as gravity? This is what Einstein attempted without success.

Einstein spent the last 30 years of his life trying to find a Unified Field Theory, but he did not succeed. Recently there had been a revival of interest in what we now call Grand Unified Theories (GUTs). But today, 50 years after Einstein's death, physicists have still not found a satisfactory answer to many of the questions Einstein raised. They continue to work on GUTs and perhaps in our lifetime they may find one.

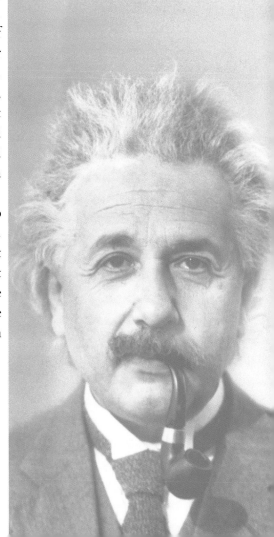

RIGHT: *Albert Einstein died in 1955, still searching for a theory that would successfully combine gravity and electromagnetism – a Grand Unified Theory that would finally explain everything in the Universe right from its very beginnings. Fifty years on, scientists are still searching....*

TIMELINE

1687	Isaac Newton develops the first theory of gravity
1879	Albert Einstein is born
1886	Heinrich Hertz generates electromagnetic waves
1887	Albert Michelson and Edward Morley conduct their experiment to determine the existence of ether
1895	Wilhelm Röntgen discovers X-rays
1896	Henri Becquerel discovers radioactivity
1897	J. J. Thomson discovers the electron
1898	H. G. Wells publishes *The War of the Worlds*, in which he predicts the development of atomic weapons
1903	Einstein marries Mileva Maric
1905	Einstein publishes his Special Theory of Relativity; he also outlines his ideas about the photoelectric effect
1908	Einstein starts teaching at the University of Bern
1909	Einstein moves to the University of Zürich
1911	Ernest Rutherford suggests the existence of the proton
1914	Einstein moves back to Germany to work at the University of Berlin
1915	Einstein publishes his General Theory of Relativity
1919	Arthur Eddington measures the deflection of light from a star around the Sun during the eclipse; Einstein marries Elsa Löwenthal
1921	Einstein is awarded the Nobel Prize for his discovery of the photoelectric effect
1927	Scientists propose the Big Bang theory for the creation of the Universe
1932	Einstein leaves Germany for the United States; James Chadwick discovers the neutron
1938	Nuclear fission becomes possible
1939	Einstein writes to President Roosevelt, warning of the dangers of developing an atomic bomb
1942	The Manhattan Project is launched
1945	The first atomic bombs are dropped on the Japanese cities of Hiroshima and Nagasaki
1955	Einstein dies
1967	Pulsars are discovered, proving the existence of black holes in space

GLOSSARY

ANTIPARTICLE A particle that has exactly the same mass but the opposite charge of another particle. All particles, such as protons, neutrons and electrons, have an antiparticle: antiprotons, antineutrons and positrons.

ANTI-SEMITISM A strong dislike or cruel treatment of people who follow the Jewish faith.

ATOM The smallest part of an element that has all the properties of that element.

ATOMIC BOMB Any nuclear weapon that uses fission to release energy; atomic bombs use either uranium or plutonium.

ATOMIC SPECTRUM The unique range of colours emitted by the atoms of each element.

BLACK HOLE An object, such as a dying star, whose gravity is so strong that even light cannot escape.

CHEMICAL ELEMENT A substance that cannot be separated into a simpler substance.

CHEMICAL ENERGY Energy released as a result of chemical reactions.

COMPOUND A substance formed by the combination of two or more chemical elements.

CO-ORDINATE A number or measurement that identifies an object's position.

ELECTRIC FIELD A force field caused by an electric charge.

ELECTROMAGNETIC SPECTRUM The range of frequencies of electromagnetic radiation, such as radio waves, visible light and X-rays.

ELECTRON The particle that orbits the nucleus of an atom and carries the negative electric charge.

ETHER The imaginary 'material' that scientists once thought light must travel through in space.

FISSION A process in which the nucleus of heavier elements such as uranium splits into two chunks, releasing a lot of energy. The process is an example of Einstein's famous equation, $E=mc^2$. Fission is the physical process used to provide the power in nuclear weapons.

FUSION A process in which nuclei of light atoms such as hydrogen combine. In the process, mass is converted to energy according to $E=mc^2$. Fusion occurs in the Sun to produce heat and light. It is also the process involved in some kinds of nuclear weapons.

HYDROGEN BOMB A weapon that uses nuclear fusion to release enormous amounts of energy.

ISOTOPE An atom of the same element, but with a different number of neutrons in the nucleus, and therefore a different mass.

KINETIC ENERGY The energy a body has because of its motion.

MAGNETIC FIELD A region of space near a magnetised body where magnetic forces can be felt.

MASS A measure of how much matter something contains.

MOLECULE An atom or a group of atoms that can exist on their own, held together by chemical bonds.

NEUTRON A particle found in the nucleus with no electric charge. It is the counterpart to the proton. Today physicists think that neutrons are made of quarks.

PATENT A document granting an inventor rights to his or her invention.

PHOTOELECTRIC EFFECT When an electron is emitted from a surface after being hit by electromagnetic radiation.

PROTON The particle in the nucleus of an atom containing the positive electric charge.

PULSAR A neutron star, near the end of its life, which gives off radiation that looks as though it is 'pulsing', or flashing on and off.

QUANTUM A unit, or packet, of electro-magnetic energy.

QUANTUM MECHANICS The study of physics on tiny scales, such as subatomic particles.

QUARK A particle that makes up protons and neutrons; the other group of these elementary particles is leptons. These particles affect each other through a range of forces.

RADIATION Energy that is transmitted in the form of waves, rays or particles; visible light is a form of radiation.

REFRACTION The bending of a beam of light as it passes from one medium to another, e.g. from air to glass.

RELATIVITY A collection of theories first suggested by Albert Einstein, which made several predictions about light, time, mass and motion, and which form the basis of our understanding of the Universe today.

SPACE-TIME Four-dimensional space used to represent the Universe in quantum physics. There are three dimensions of space and one of time.

SPECTROSCOPY The study of spectra – the range of colours emitted by an object.

SPEED OF LIGHT The speed of light is nearly 300,000 kps when it travels through empty space, a vacuum. It is the same for everyone who measures it.

TIME DILATION The phenomenon whereby two people travelling in opposite directions at steady speed, close to the speed of light, will think each other's clocks are running slow.

VACUUM A region where there is no free matter. Space is a vacuum.

VELOCITY Distance travelled in unit time – for example, kilometres per hour.

WAVELENGTH The distance between the peaks of two successive waves.

X-RAYS A form of electromagnetic radiation with very short wavelength and high energy.

FURTHER INFORMATION

WEB SITES

http://science.howstuffworks.com/relativity.htm
The section of the How Stuff Works site that explains all about Einstein and relativity, including information on the properties of the Universe and whether or not time travel might actually be possible. Elsewhere on the site you can find information on the properties of light and many other associated subjects.

www.albert-einstein.org/
A good site with links to information about Einstein, his life and works. You can even learn how to think like Einstein.

BOOKS

Albert Einstein by Saviour Pirotta: Scientists Who Made History, Hodder Wayland, 2002
Albert Einstein by Struan Reid: Groundbreakers, Heinemann Library, 2001
Einstein by Chris Oxlade: Twentieth-century History Makers, Franklin Watts, 2003
Einstein and Relativity by Paul Strathern: Big Ideas, Arrow Books, 1997
Introducing Einstein by Joseph Schwartz and Michael McGuinness: Icon Books, 2000
Spilling the Beans on Albert Einstein by Mick Gower: Miles Kelly Publishing, 2000

INDEX